T0311430

SOCIAL TRANSPARENCY: PROJECTS ON HOUSING

Michael Maltzan

with essays by Hilary Sample, Níall McLaughlin, & Florian Idenburg

A PROJECT OF THE HOUSING STUDIOS AT
COLUMBIA GSAPP, DIRECTED BY HILARY SAMPLE

INTRODUCTION BY AMALE ANDRAOS

EDITED BY JAMES GRAHAM

COLUMBIA BOOKS ON ARCHITECTURE
AND THE CITY, 2016

The GSAPP Transcripts series is a curated record of the major events that take place at the Columbia University Graduate School of Architecture, Planning, and Preservation. Embracing the simple idea that publication is the act of making something public, these books form a channel through which the discourse internal to the school enters the public arena of architectural media and ideas, in the form of edited talks and symposia. In each case, the original lectures and discussions at the core of these books are augmented with supplementary material, additional imagery, and critical commentary, expanding their debates and provocations beyond the confines of the lecture hall.

For digital editions of some GSAPP Transcripts, visit arch.columbia.edu/books/reader.

Transcripts on Housing is a subset of the GSAPP Transcripts series, in collaboration with the M.Arch Housing Studios at Columbia University GSAPP.

Rem Koolhaas
Preservation Is Overtaking Us
with a supplement by
Jorge Otero-Pailos (2014)

Yvonne Farrell
and Shelley McNamara
Dialogue and Translation:
Grafton Architects
with an essay by
Kenneth Frampton (2014)

2000+: The Urgencies of
Architectural Theory
ed. James Graham (2015)

Group Efforts: Changing
Public Space
ed. Gavin Browning, with an
essay by Mabel Wilson (2015)

Angelo Bucci
The Dissolution of Buildings
with an essay by
Kenneth Frampton (2015)

Michael Maltzan
Social Transparency:
Projects on Housing
with essays by Hilary Sample,
Níall McLaughlin, and Florian
Idenburg (2016)

"Architecture's power lies in its engagement with the real."

INTRODUC-TION
Amale Andraos

Architecture's power lies in its engagement with the real, and for the past twenty years, Michael Maltzan has been one of the discipline's leaders in shaping what that engagement might look like. Whether designed for cultural institutions, private clients, or marginalized urban populations who are too rarely addressed by practicing architects, Maltzan's work has been at once thoughtful, inspiring, and radically inventive as it recasts new possibilities for how the built environment can better answer fundamental questions about how we live.

It may seem curious that an architecture school in New York would turn to an Angeleno for ideas on housing, given the nearly opposite role these cities play in assumed histories of urban development in America. But as Maltzan's work shows us, it is high time to upend such binaries and to think more collaboratively—across continents and across disciplines—about the way architecture locates itself within the physical and social fabrics of the urban landscape. Since 1975, the housing studio has been a fundamental part of Columbia's M.Arch curriculum (given New York's history of compelling precedents and pressing needs), but the work of housing is not just local; it is national and global as well. As the current director of our housing studios, Hilary Sample has been instrumental in expanding the school's sites of inquiry in order to look at this important architectural question across a number of global contexts. In bringing Maltzan to the school to speak about his work, she has invited us not only to learn from one of the field's most agile designers, but to learn from the particular context of Los Angeles and expand beyond it.

Maltzan's four buildings for the Skid Row Housing Trust in Los Angeles are a truly remarkable complement to his larger body of work. They insist on the fundamental dignity of the at-risk or the dispossessed; they create dynamic and dramatic moments in the city with minimal means; they offer remarkable spatial and typological innovations. Michael Maltzan's projects on housing inspire a sense of pleasure together with a sense of urgency, and so it is with both pleasure and urgency that we publish this lecture and accompanying essays.

"Maltzan's housing projects speak of our common need to situate ourselves and participate in public life."

STREET LIFE
Níall
McLaughlin

Skid Row, Los Angeles, 2015.

The name Skid Row has been immortalized in myth and music as both a place and a state of being. It is the address associated with the bottom rung of life's ladder, the dead-end destination for the hopeless. The original Skid Row was probably in Seattle and it got its name from the corduroy wooden tracks used to haul heavy lumber to the timber yards. The area around the yards became associated with the darker aspects of transient immigrant life; they became a haven for grease monkeys, vagrants, pimps, and grifters.

The area known as Skid Row in Los Angeles is a 50-block section of Downtown. It is bounded by the Historic Core and Little Tokyo and it partly overlays the Downtown Industrial District. Its origins lie in the industrial developments that grew up to service L.A.'s agricultural hinterland reached from the nearby rail yards. The seasonal nature of the work drew in a combination of short-term workers and rail crews on layover; small hotels suited to single male migrant workers serviced them. A scattering of bars, brothels, and religious missions vied for the attentions of this lonely constituency. The combination of transient accommodation and available vice set the deep structure for the district, and has persisted beyond many of the original industrial functions that generated it. By the 1930s, the place had an established character based on cheap hotels and the sorts of services and commerce that attended them. The Great Depression brought in a new population of destitute farmers, many of whom were alcoholics, who had abandoned home and family. The end of the war in Vietnam saw a new influx of residents, often traumatized and addicted to drugs other than alcohol.

At regular intervals, the L.A. city authorities would attempt to clear the area out in highly publicized campaigns of arrest and intimidation. Although these were publicly popular, they did little to change the underlying structures and the homeless population of the area continued to grow. The intractable persistence of this condition is astonishing. In 1947 an *Evening Independent* correspondent wrote, "a high class criminal wouldn't be caught dead in this area. It draws cheap grifters and floaters like a magnet. It holds 9,000 transients at all times—bums, panhandlers, small time crooks looking for a quick buck." Today Skid Row has one of the highest concentrations of homeless people in the United States. A survey dating to 2012 suggests 8,000 people in single-occupancy hotel rooms, 2,000 in transitional accommodation, and up to 4,000 living on the pavement.

In the 1960s the authorities attempted to control the population by regulating the cheap hotels using legislation related to fire codes. Many hotels were closed down or demolished. These code revisions constituted a 50 percent decrease in the housing stock for the whole area. The policy was reversed in the 1970s when it was suggested that residential facilities should be preserved and enhanced with the addition of necessary services such as clinics. This more enlightened policy had the unfortunate effect of turning Skid Row into a place where other cities in L.A. County began dumping their unwanted citizens. Discharged mental health and hospital patients were unloaded into the area from considerable distances; in 2007 a major national health provider was taken to court for depositing a patient wearing nothing but hospital robes on the pavement from a taxi. "Greyhound therapy" became known as a phrase hospitals used for a one-way bus ticket to Skid Row.

If Skid Row was a uniquely local phenomenon in certain ways, it pointed to a broader national malaise in others. It became a battleground for civil liberties activists, law enforcement agencies, city authorities, and service providers. The pressures on the area increased further as the overall development of Downtown began pushing property prices up in the area. Coffee shops, galleries, and loft developments started to appear on the fringes of this purgatory. The police attempted another clearout in 2006, based on the "broken windows theory," a form of police intimidation and cleansing given thin academic credence. Broken windows and loitering were seen to point to disorder and therefore a threshold to serious crime. Saner voices argued that broken windows are merely indicative of poverty. People were cleared out of the area with no destination in mind. This simply exported the problem, with the most vulnerable populations separated from the services they depended upon. Since then, a new and tentative compromise has formed with the City saying that it will not clear out homeless people without providing additional homes in the area.

The Skid Row Housing Trust (SRHT) was set up in the late 1980s to provide permanently supportive housing for formerly homeless individuals. In the 1990s, they began refurbishing old dilapidated hotels using talented local architectural practices. They realized that stable accommodation only worked when combined with essential services, and they developed a building model combining single-occupancy rooms, communal facilities, and services such as mental health treatment, substance abuse recovery, money management, and benefits advocacy. They began to target the most vulnerable people living on the street. Their work constitutes a criticism of the whole city by reassembling a complete set of homeless services system in one place. From the beginning, they advocated high quality architecture on the basis that it establishes the basic coordinates of a dignified settled environment for people who have lost trust in the idea of home; it also advertises to the neighborhood and the broader city that these people are here and that they have a viable identity in this place. This combination of inhabitation and representation is the basis for the architect's brief.

Over the past ten years, no architect has engaged this work in Los Angeles with as much commitment and ingenuity as Michael Maltzan, whose firm is now completing its fourth building for the SRHT. Well known for a wide range of exquisite private dwellings and thoughtful public projects, his career has followed a familiar and enviable trajectory from bespoke houses to cultural institutions and major pieces of civic infrastructure. In this context, the design of low-cost housing for the previously homeless is a unique challenge. Maltzan insists that while this building type has its own architectural problems, it is designed within the practice according to the same values and systems as any other commission.

The first of these projects, the Rainbow Apartments, is built as a conventional urban block with communal services at ground level and individual rooms over five stories above. The upper accommodations are arranged around a U-shaped courtyard set at right angles to the street. The courtyard, established at first-floor level, is reached by a grand stair from the entrance and is surrounded by deck-access balconies serving individual rooms at each level. Maltzan sees the courtyard as establishing a common zone between the pleasures and perils of the street and the more isolated safety of the individual room; in the context of an individual in transition from homelessness to more permanent dwelling, this becomes the spatial crux of the architectural proposal. It is conceived in terms of views between balconies and rooms, but also in how the courtyard frames the sky and connects to the street. The architect then establishes a simple visual language based on plain stucco walls enlivened by colored window reveals and openings, as though a sober suit has opened to reveal a sumptuous lining.

Rainbow Apartments, model showing interior courtyard. → fig. 009

The next project, the Carver Apartments, is built about a mile from the center of Skid Row beside the I-10 Freeway—a position that allows it to be read as a beacon on the scale of the larger city while obliging it to address noise. The section is broadly similar to the Rainbow project with ground-floor services and a grand stair rising to a central atrium flanked by open walkways. The plan, however, is based on a circular geometry with rooms radiating from the center. Every room is turned slightly towards the perimeter, giving a twisting centrifugal quality to the figure of each floor plate.

The circular form is undoubtedly informed by environmental factors, but this cylindrical beacon by the freeway also draws the design into dialogue with other celebrated buildings in

L.A., in particular Welton Becket's Capitol Records Building. Instead of Becket's suggestive horizontal canopies, we have a vertical rotational unfolding, beautifully reminiscent in plan and elevation of Aalto's housing tower in Lucerne. The torsion is taken into the circular atrium by a screen of vertical fins that establish some distance between the individual rooms and the common atrium. This does something to offset the much higher concentration of

New Carver Apartments, seen next to the I-10 Freeway to Santa Monica. → fig. 013

space created by the central circular form. In all its virtuosity, this project moves in the balance from artless inhabitation toward an emphatic and singular representation. At the very limit of Skid Row, this building marks the presence of supportive housing for individual homeless with a powerful rhetorical presence.

Star Apartments, the third project in this suite, again combines essential services, communal facilities, and individual rooms. Here the common space of the atrium is turned outwards as a continuous veranda at podium level. The prefabricated rooms are elaborately held overhead like a suspended kasbah. The key contrast is between the enclosed court and the outward-looking balcony; the safety, sociability, and intimacy of the communal spaces seems central to the success of this transitional building type. "Broken-windows" policing discourages people from loitering in groups on the pavement; such disorganized conviviality is seen as a threshold to crime. Here it is intended that groups will loiter one floor above the

Star Apartments, building as city block. → fig. 025

15

Níall McLaughlin

pavement, establishing a sociable presence protected from, but participating in, the life of the street.

The architect has said that he would like these projects to be read together, and this book gives us the opportunity to do just that. The formal virtuosity of each composition displays Maltzan's talents and suggests that architecture can give pleasure and dignity to all of us. They also announce the enduring presence of transient and marginalized people in this area, thereby giving them a much-needed sense of legitimacy. I hope that the different spatial experiments—linking and articulating ground planes, common sheltered space, and private rooms— will become subjects for further reflection and analysis. Maltzan's housing projects speak of our common need to situate ourselves and participate in public life.

"If you could imagine connecting all of these different projects, then perhaps 'the project' is all of them together with the smaller increments beginning to add up to a kind of remapping of the city itself."
→ pp. 89–90

An earlier version of this essay was published as "Street Life: Michael Maltzan's Social Housing in Los Angeles," in the *Architectural Review* (September 16, 2013), http://www.architectural-review.com/today/street-life-michael-maltzans-social-housing-in-los-angeles/8652420.article, and is reprinted here with the permission of the publisher.

"Reducing the presence of those things we usually call 'architecture' demands that we return to what is most *effective* about architecture and the way it frames social relationships."

SOCIAL TRANSPAR- ENCY Michael Maltzan

Michael Maltzan at Columbia University's Graduate School of Architecture, Planning, and Preservation, April 15, 2015.

Housing is often thought of as a very specific part of the discipline of architecture, having its own forms of technical knowledge and its own particularities of building code and economy. But at the same time, going all the way back to the very beginnings of modernism, housing has historically been one of the most expansive typologies within the field, witnessing a type of progress that goes well beyond technical and functional challenges, and in fact represents culture and society at the most profound levels. It manifests an incredible complexity of architectural ideas, touching on social, economic, political, aesthetic, and urban questions. For that reason, our office doesn't think about housing as separate from the rest of what we do. On the contrary, we are intensely interested in how housing reinforces our other work, as well as how the other work fuels our thinking about housing, so that housing becomes a deeply integrated and influential part of our practice.

In Los Angeles, where we are based, the relationship between housing and the city at large is still emerging. Los Angeles is for the most part a city that grew up after World War II. And like most postwar suburban settlements across the United States, it is primarily made up of single-family housing. From the air, if you squint, the vast carpet of freestanding houses can seem to add up to one big housing project. On the ground, the city's psychology is still very suburban, very much about the individual. But like a lot of contemporary cities, Los Angeles—which covers more area than most cities in the world—is now becoming more

Michael Maltzan

Suburban development under construction in Lakewood, California, southeast of downtown Los Angeles, 1950; photograph by William A. Garnett.

and more dense, and apartment buildings and condominiums, forms we have to understand as collective housing, are becoming increasingly prevalent. While this is partially owing to a steady influx of new residents, it is also the case that sprawl has begun to hit its topographical and practical limits in terms of the city's sheer extension. As Los Angeles evolves in ways that the single-family-house model doesn't easily sustain, the city's social and cultural interests are starting to take on a more collective and connected character. This has also challenged architecture, because a limited range of existing housing types offers few productive models to depend on or refer to.

I had wanted to design housing for a long time and never had the chance to. Not much housing was actually being done in Southern California, and most of the developers doing housing weren't interested in hiring architecture offices like mine. When I was in school, housing studios were a core part of architectural education, as they are here at Columbia, and those studios were influential—not only in terms of housing as a design problem, but also in terms of architectural history. We were rediscovering modernism at the time, and it was eye-opening to see how housing had been a source of seemingly endless experimentation: housing projects were structural projects, conceptual projects, planning projects, and spatial projects all at once. I believed, maybe naively, that housing was something an architect inevitably did. When we finally had the opportunity to do that kind of project, we came to grips with the real lack of interesting prototypes in our own city. That forced me, in the positive sense, to go back to what I learned as a student about housing and its relationship to modernism, and what fascinated me most was the fact that housing was the essential typology of modernism.

I'd like to talk about five housing projects our office has worked on, four of which have been realized in collaboration with the Skid Row Housing Trust; but I want to start with a single-family house. We don't do a lot of houses, but I'm interested in them because that microcosm of the single-family house can be a focused experiment on the mechanisms that architecture can employ to create social environments. They are like little cities in and of themselves: your entire life takes place

in a house. They may be single-family, but
they aren't single-use programs. They contain
an enormous amount of complexity and history,
while also representing our ambitions about
how we want to live today.

This project, the Pittman Dowell Residence in
La Crescenta, completed in 2009, sits at the
furthest edge of what has become the quintes-
sential and very characteristic single-family
residential sprawl of Los Angeles, more than 15
miles from the downtown core. The 6-acre site
in the foothills of the San Gabriel Mountains
already contained a house by Richard Neutra,
the Dorothy Serulnic Residence built in 1953.
Neutra had convinced the client to cut three
building pads into the site, one for the house
he designed and two spares; our project took
on one of those pads.

I think Neutra was
trying to be practi-
cal, thinking that the
owners might want to
subdivide the prop-
erty at some point,
but I also think he
was always interested
in a type of social-
ist enterprise. Even
single-family houses,

Pittman Dowell Residence, La
Crescenta, California, completed
2009. → fig. 001

in his thinking, were meant to be a part of a
larger collective. It was rare that Neutra ever
designed a house without considering its possible existence among four or five other houses,
which he would typically design himself, so
maybe it was in part a business strategy. But
the single-family house wasn't as interesting

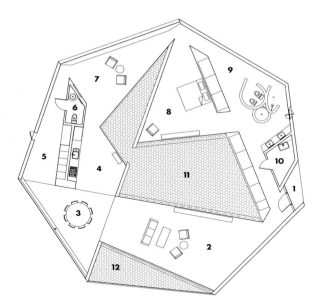

Floor Plan

1 Entry
2 Living Room
3 Dining Room
4 Kitchen
5 Office
6 Powder Room
7 Library
8 Bedroom
9 Master Bath
10 Utility Closet
11 Courtyard
12 Balcony

0
0
6

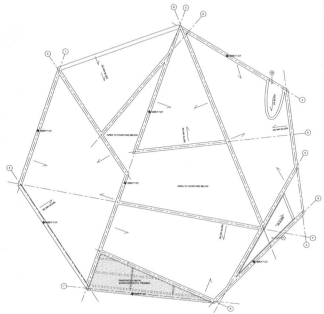

Roof Plan

to Neutra as its social and collective mechanisms, and this is something that we want to
respond to in our work.

Our clients, who were the second owners of the
Serulnic Residence, wanted to keep the Neutra
house. At the same time, it had become for them
an historic artifact; it didn't really relate
to the way they lived. They started by ques-
tioning its lightness and transparency. Given
that the mountains can get very windy and cold
("cold" for Angelinos, at least), the house
could feel like you were camping out. They
commissioned us to design a second house that
would feel more permanent and be more inward
looking, less directed outward to the elements.
This led me to an observation that the kind
of transparency in a Neutra house, a modernist

**Richard Neutra, Dorothy Serulnic Residence, 1953;
photograph by Julius Shulman, 1955.**

idea, maybe even a romantic idea, is not necessarily a contemporary idea.

The Serulnic Residence represented a moment in which dissolving the line between inside and outside was philosophically and structurally essential to Neutra's work—literally the spatial problem that preoccupied him.

But perhaps this gesture no longer aligns with what we need from a house or architecture generally. Our own time is one of enormous social transparency and connection to things around us. Our private lives are more and more blurred with our public lives, as the transparency that was almost a moral imperative for Neutra becomes increasingly fraught. I have grown more interested in how to achieve a kind of socially connected visibility while also exploring what it means to be private. Today, without ever leaving home, we exist in multiple places simultaneously: wherever we are, we're almost always connected to something else. Even if those connections aren't physical, the spaces in which they occur are nevertheless connected to one another in a very real way, and this is represented in archi-tecture. I would say that this simultaneity is the most compel-ling spatial challenge confronting archi-tects now, the spatial characteristic that perhaps best defines our time.

Pittman Dowell Residence, with Serulnic Residence at left. ← fig. 002

The house we designed is almost the total alter ego of Neutra's Serulnic Residence, and yet the seeds of a kind of simultaneity were already embedded in the site by way of the relationship Neutra imagined among the three houses he plotted there. The original house is connected to the new one by a single large tree, the iconic element that became the mediator between the two. While the Neutra house was wrapped in glass, our design is opaque on the outside, with just a few apertures through which you see in and see out. Light enters primarily through skylights and an internal courtyard. The house sits like an object on one of the pads Neutra cut. The outside is solid and opaque, but the inside is almost completely transparent. The inside walls are mostly glass, and most of the rooms don't have dividers between them. This means that when you're inside the living room, the courtyard,

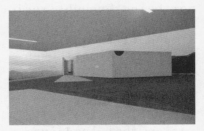

Pittman Dowell Residence, an object on a building pad. ← fig. 003

Pittman Dowell Residence, view of interior courtyard. ← fig. 004

Pittman Dowell Residence, interior. ← fig. 005

kitchen, bathroom, and master bedroom are all
very visible. It's as if we took the Serulnic
Residence, which has its fireplace and dense
core in the middle and glass on the outside,
and folded it in on itself, with all of the
exterior transparency, all of the public-ness
now being brought inside the private world of
the house. You move
around it in a clock-
wise spiral, although
you can shortcut the
spiral at points
across the courtyard.
In plan, the spiraling
motion that leads you
into the living room
takes you by the open-
ing to the bathroom
first, so the most
private place in the
house actually belongs
to the most public
space of the entry.
You move clockwise
through the living
room, the dining room,

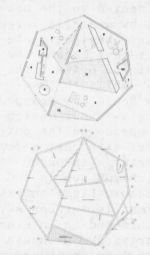

Pittman Dowell Residence, floor and roof plans. ← fig. 006

a small kitchen, an office, and eventually,
the bedroom and bathroom, bringing you back to
the beginning.

RAINBOW APARTMENTS

Our office began working on multi-unit housing ten years ago. The first of these projects
was the Rainbow Apartments (2006) in downtown
Los Angeles for the Skid Row Housing Trust. The

Housing Trust always names their projects after an apartment building in the neighborhood that has been torn down, as a way of connecting new housing to a longer history and raising awareness

Rainbow Apartments, for the Skid Row Housing Trust, Los Angeles, California, completed 2006. → fig. 007

about housing in a city that rarely looks back. Up to this time, the Housing Trust had for the most part been developing hotel-like Single Room Occupancy (SRO) buildings, transitional housing where the homeless could spend a couple of nights, perhaps up to a month. We were invited to design the Rainbow Apartments, eighty-nine units, at a moment when the Housing Trust was transitioning from the SRO model to a Permanent Supportive Housing (PSH) model in which residents could potentially live the rest of their lives if they chose to. It was housing conceived as "home." The other essential aspect of Permanent Supportive Housing is that it includes vital social infrastructure for the inhabitants.

With each of the four housing projects I will be talking about here, the building was oriented toward a particular homeless population. Among the residents of the Rainbow Apartments, about 75 percent are HIV positive. Our second project for the Housing Trust was for elderly homeless; the third was for people with chronic physical, and in some cases, mental disabilities; the fourth was for formerly homeless veterans. Each community requires a complex set of services, and in the past these people would have to commute, often over long distances, to see their doctors, social workers, psychologists—basically to access the infrastructure that supports their lives. That fact of being constantly out on the street in search of supportive services has led to high levels of recidivism and instability. The things that kept a lot of these individuals in trouble are still out there, and they are harder to confront in the absence of a supportive community. The thinking that has evolved in the social services sector in response to the minimal gains achieved by the old system is that moving services, doctors, and caseworkers into the housing creates a greater likelihood of building more stable lives. Consequently, each of these housing projects takes on greater programmatic complexity, effectively becoming a community within the city—the kind of community that its inhabitants have lacked for much of their lives.

The Rainbow Apartments were an enormous learning step for us as an office and very challenging from a cost standpoint. Rainbow is a U-shaped building with a single-loaded corridor on the outside of the courtyard. This was a way to take advantage of the Southern California climate. The single-loaded

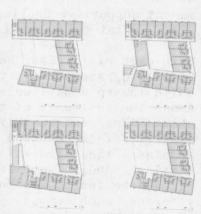

Rainbow Apartments, floor plans.
→ fig. 008

corridor has another function here as well. To be eligible for this type of housing, a person must be "chronically homeless," which means having been on the street for ten years. I would have imagined that six months could qualify a person as chronically homeless, but imagine, ten years. For many of the people coming into the building, their entire psychology is based on being "in public" all of the time. Homelessness obviously doesn't afford the luxury of having a private world within a public world. Many of these individuals have built up shells around themselves that make it difficult for them to relate in a more social way. They have lost their capacity to relate in public, which is something most of us take for granted. Breaking open the usual double-loaded corridor that you find in housing projects is a very simple design move, but the effect is powerful. It means that whenever you come in or go out of your apartment, you enter the communal space of the courtyard. You cannot go up in the elevator, walk down the double-loaded corridor, and disappear into your unit. Instead you have to become part of this semi-public world, even if it is for just a few moments.

Rainbow Apartments, model showing interior courtyard. → fig. 009

But we have to be realistic about architecture's ability to create wholesale social change. Historically, the thinking has been that building collective housing would guarantee transformation in social conditions. This is one of the romantic myths of modernism. There are many, many factors that go into making true social change. But at the same time, architecture can't stand back. There is the potential for agency. Architecture can use its tools in focused ways to change the way that a community relates to itself and to the city, for instance. The Rainbow Apartments project became an example of a situation in which architecture could assume an active role in the realization of sociological and psychological benefits that the Housing Trust is trying to make possible for its residents.

We lost 50 to 75 percent of what we normally think of as architecture in this building. The interior screen around the courtyard that was part of the original design was value-engineered out, for example. Materials are often used in a way that imports a kind of fanciness to a building, and the use of materials in that way, it seems to me, has a very short shelf life. Before long, something that was designed to look contemporary feels dated. I'm more interested in subverting that and making the materials less apparent, so that the forms and relationships they construct have to stand on their own. I've come to think of color as a material itself, in a way, because it can have as much of a transformative effect as other

Rainbow Apartments, model.
→ fig. 010

treatments. Nonetheless, some of the coloration got trimmed from the Rainbow budget. By the time we were done, we were negotiating whether there would be two or three screws in the door hinges.

On the other hand, reducing the presence of those things we usually call "architecture" demands that we return to what is most effective about architecture and the way it frames social relationships. Instead of pointing to the formal aspects that we couldn't hang on to, these requirements ask us to step back and reevaluate what is most foundational and different about our design. This is one of the functions of housing studios in schools, the ones I took and the ones you do here at Columbia. They involve stepping back and looking at how the most fundamental elements of architecture—courtyards or double-loaded corridors, prosaic things like that—have evolved historically and ultimately come to have substantial agency in the lived world.

The interiors of the Rainbow units were also a real challenge, especially in some of the smaller units. Housing codes have changed a great deal over the past decades. ADA bathrooms have gotten larger and larger, to the point that they're almost the largest room in these very compact apartments. The strategy we

Rainbow Apartments, typical interior of studio apartment. → fig. 011

employed was to design in the capability for all of the bathrooms to be converted to full ADA, although in the beginning, only 20 percent would actually meet those standards. All are constructed to the required dimensions with blocking in the walls so that grab bars and other equipment can be added later. Since the basic business model for buildings like these doesn't allow you to expand much beyond 250 to 300 square feet per unit, it becomes difficult to create large spaces for living when there are such prescriptive technical and code-based requirements. It demands that there be a certain leanness to the building, but it pushes you to imagine how you might make something like a bathroom or a kitchen more efficient and also more generous than they usually are, so they come to play a larger role in the space of the unit.

Many architects who have worked with this type of affordable housing do one project and then say, "Thank you, that was a lot of fun." They feel like they've done their turn and don't pursue it further. Within the framework of a normal architecture practice this work is hard. For us, though, it was important to build on what we'd learned from the "failures" we'd just grappled with. The only way of becoming more successful at difficult buildings like these is to transfer the lessons about what does and doesn't work into the next projects. I asked the Housing Trust if we could do at least two more projects with them, and they said, "Yes."

NEW CARVER APARTMENTS (2009)

Our second project, the New Carver Apartments, wasn't slated for the Skid Row district but rather a site right next to the Interstate 10 freeway that runs through downtown Los Angeles to Santa Monica in an increasingly visible district of the city. The Housing Trust was interested in moving out into other parts of the city to meet the homeless communities it serves in a way that emphasizes a broader presence throughout the city, rather than confining its activity to a specific area. Their incredible success in developing projects in Skid Row was starting to create, incrementally, the equivalent of enormous residential projects familiar to the postwar boom in public housing in cities across the United States, which continues to be such a fraught topic. Rather than build out Skid Row to serve and contain a single community, their hope, urbanistically, has been to connect and weave these communities into the city at large.

Carver sits only about 20 feet from the massive Interstate 10 freeway and, ironically, at the end of Hope Street. In Los Angeles, freeways are in many ways our version of the front yard, our most visible public space, characterized by people passing by. Our

New Carver Apartments, for the Skid Row Housing Trust, Los Angeles, California, completed 2009. → fig. 012

office was trying to use that infrastructure

as a Main Street of sorts, on which to stage a visual encounter between people moving through the city and the mostly invisible homeless. The problem with infrastructure, I think, is that for too long it has been conceived as a mono-culture in that it does exactly one thing, in this case it moves cars, but gives little else back to the city. In our project, given the improbable proximity to the freeway infrastruc-ture, I was trying to suggest that one might imagine the building as a part of the freeway, its concrete walls and columns indistinguish-able from those of the transportation system. By getting that close to the freeway, maybe one could imagine getting closer and closer and closer, finally closing that gap and integrat-ing infrastructure and housing. Or at least the "monoculture" of infrastructure could start to give way to a more complex relationship between space and community—maybe even giving rise to a "multi-culture."

The building is more or less circular, so it has this quality that makes it feel like it spins as you drive by it. But the form also came from specific technical concerns. One of the problems with using single-loaded corridors is that they increase the amount

New Carver Apartments, seen next to the I-10 Freeway to Santa Monica. → fig. 013

of exterior surface area, and the exterior is, generally, the most expensive thing in a build-ing. What we were interested in, in an almost

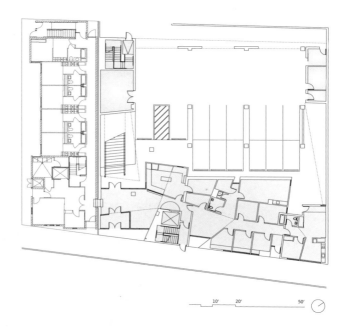

10' 20' 50'

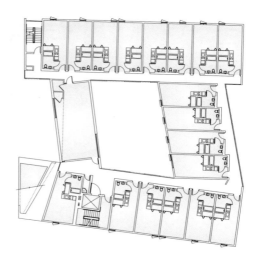

10' 20' 50'

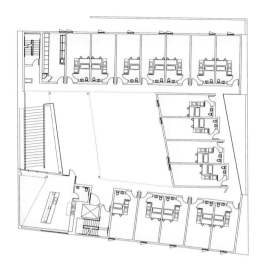

10' 20'   50'

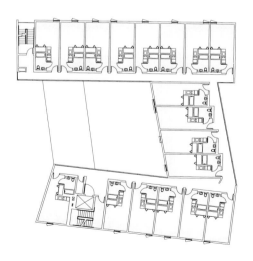

10' 20'   50'

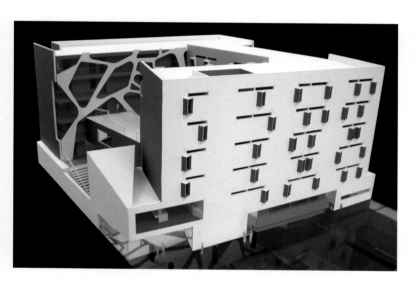

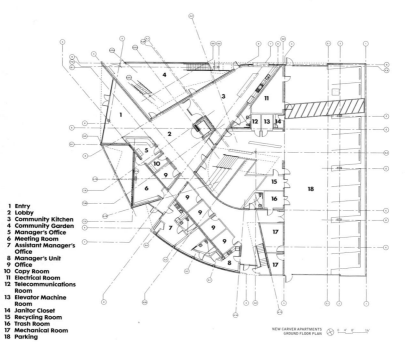

1 Entry
2 Lobby
3 Community Kitchen
4 Community Garden
5 Manager's Office
6 Meeting Room
7 Assistant Manager's
    Office
8 Manager's Unit
9 Office
10 Copy Room
11 Electrical Room
12 Telecommunications
    Room
13 Elevator Machine
    Room
14 Janitor Closet
15 Recycling Room
16 Trash Room
17 Mechanical Room
18 Parking

NEW CARVER APARTMENTS
GROUND FLOOR PLAN   0 4' 8'   16'

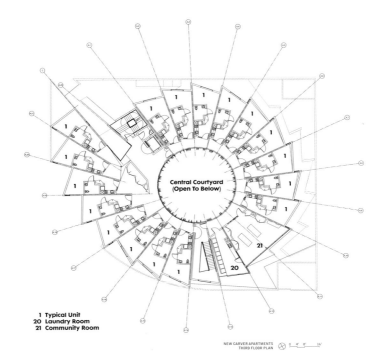

Central Courtyard
(Open To Below)

21

20

1 Typical Unit
20 Laundry Room
21 Community Room

NEW CARVER APARTMENTS
THIRD FLOOR PLAN

0   4'   8'   16'

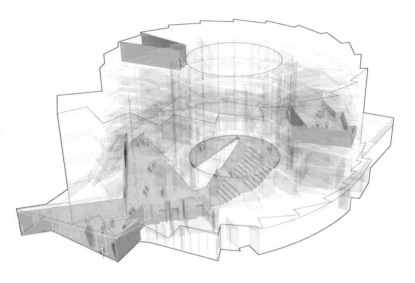

hypothetical way, was what kind of shape would create the maximum interior floor plates with the minimum circumferential exterior surface, and that turns out to be the circle. The shape was also driven by acoustical considerations. While the visibility from the freeway was a real asset, the noise was an enormous problem, and triple-glazing the windows and building acoustic walls would obviously just add to the costs. But every foot you move away from a sound source sees a drop in decibels, and the circular shape had the benefit of presenting the smallest piece of facade to the highway.

The ground floor contains many of the same supportive services as the Rainbow Apartments, as well as communal facilities like a kitchen, a common room, spaces for medical professionals and caseworkers to meet with residents, and a large outdoor courtyard. The form of the building as it meets the street creates a series of angled, perspectival "skewers" through the building. As you're moving around the ground floor, you're looking through or under the freeway

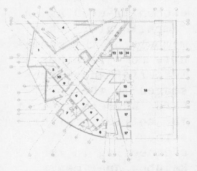

New Carver Apartments, ground floor under construction and ground floor plan. ← figs. O14 & O15

overpass as well as the connecting surface streets. As you get up inside the building, there is a central courtyard surrounded by a single-loaded corridor. The ninety-seven units are organized in a fan shape, which starts to suggest that they are part of a larger collective, but breaks in the form—small indentations of a foot-and-a-half in the wall around the courtyard space—give each of the units a sense of individuality. For us, that relationship between the individual and the collective remains one of the most important issues in housing.

The courtyard is open to the elements and functions as a space for social interaction. There are generous stairs that take you up from the ground floor, which also function as a space for social encounter—even as an "amphitheater" when members of the community come together or if performances are staged in the courtyard. Whereas we lost the entire interior screen to value-engineering in the Rainbow Apartments, I was determined that wouldn't happen here.

New Carver Apartments, amphitheater in the interior courtyard and upper level plan. ← figs. O16 & O17

The interior screen was extremely important, so what we did was merge the design elements with necessary functional elements around the interior of the courtyard. The balconies are all hung with steel rods, and roof drains come down through the interior of the courtyard. We also had a methane problem on the site, so some of the vertical articulations are

New Carver Apartments, functional fins lining the interior courtyard. ← fig. 018

actually a series of methane vents. That means that many of the fins that wrap the courtyard have functional importance and can't be removed from the building; if the interior skin is removed, the balconies fall down, the courtyard floods, the place fills up with methane. We didn't think of it as a "trick" so much as a way of saying that something like a freeway now has to do more in the city, just like the things we do as architects have to support two or three uses at once.

Community functions are distributed throughout the building rather than concentrated on the ground floor. There's a big terrace at the top with views of the city. The very important and very prosaic elements of

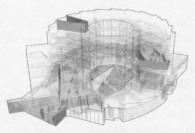

New Carver Apartments, distribution of community functions through the building. ← fig. 019

the TV room and laundry room are on the third floor, right at the level of the elevated freeway. When residents are doing laundry or watching TV, it's like they have a porch that opens on to the public space of the highway; at night it becomes a visible space that connects the community of residents to the community of drivers on I-10. This being Los Angeles, traffic is stopped fairly often, so in a city where things and lives are often dis-connected, these two communities get to see each other and thus connect. That chore-ography of a visual connection doesn't

New Carver Apartments, community room looking out over I-10. ← fig. 020

build community automatically, but at least it tries to suggest that the isolation of human beings (whether economic or physical) is some-thing that architecture can try to undermine.

STAR APARTMENTS

Our third project, the Star Apartments, 102 units on Skid Row in the shadow of downtown, is surrounded by a number of low-rise buildings with parking on their roofs. In going back to Skid Row, one of the goals of the Housing Trust was to attempt a more mixed-use approach. For New Yorkers, retail on the ground floor and housing above might not sound that strange, but in a city like Los Angeles, that's a fairly new tendency in housing. The Housing Trust relies on federal housing money, and there are regulations that say if you're in the housing business, you're not allowed to be in the commercial business. But they found a crucial loophole: if you develop a building with existing

Star Apartments, for the Skid Row Housing Trust, Los Angeles, California, completed 2014. → fig. O21

retail, you can keep that going. So they found exactly that, and gave it to us to work with. We've changed it quite a bit, but the existing building became the ground floor of our building mostly by scraping off and replacing the facade. The old building had parking up on top, which wasn't going to be so necessary for us, so we tucked the parking that we needed into the back of the building and maintained two facades of retail use. The existing structure became a podium. The

Star Apartments, existing retail development and rendering of new complex. → fig. O22

retail clinic of the Los Angeles County Health Department is among the ground floor tenants moving in, which is interesting.

Even beyond the loophole allowing developers to carry forward existing retail space, I think we increasingly have to think about the reuse of existing buildings as the city continues to densify. We too often depend on systems and the mechanics of a building to create sustainability, but it's equally important to step back and look at the way we develop sites, at what can be preserved and saved. To build on top of an existing building, we had to build a new building with its own independent structure. It started to become clear that we could create a structural tray on which we could then build the rest of the housing. It could have looked like anything, but we were interested in using that gap between old and new structure to provide a horizontal community space that could become the equivalent of the more vertical courtyards we did in the previous two projects. In this case, there is a community kitchen, eating area, offices for caseworkers, an art classroom, a general education classroom, and a computer classroom. Outdoors there is a jogging and walking track, half-court basketball, and a gym and yoga deck. All of these larger community functions that we would normally not be

Star Apartments, from Sixth Street and Maple Avenue. → fig. 023

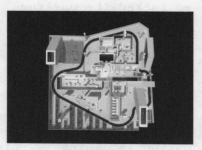

Star Apartments, plan rendering showing community programs on the elevated plinth. → fig. 024

able to fit into the building, or that would be outside of the building, are now increasingly being pulled into the building. The hope is that the residents aren't just connected to social casework or medical functions, but also to a more expansive range of education and recreation.

Most people don't think of Los Angeles as a particularly dense city, but in fact it is, just not vertically dense. But as the population continues to expand, there's also increasing pressure to create a kind of hyper-density, especially around housing. One of the goals of this project was to see just how many units we could provide, and what kind of quality of life that might present to the people who live here.

Star Apartments, building as city block. → fig. 025

From above, you can see that the building is thick with units at the perimeter and also within the interior of the block. It's almost like a city block, or even multiple city blocks, squeezed into one building. This is possible because some open space was created by the way the units are stepped in plan, allowing access to air and light,

Star Apartments, vertical spaces of the interior courtyard. → fig. 026

and also because that community space underneath provides some of the functions for the
units themselves. The result is a number of
really interesting vertical shafts through
the structure.

Given the building reuse and the density we
were trying to achieve, there was very little
space on the site for staging construction,
and because of that, we started looking at pre-
fabrication. For Los
Angeles, this is the
first multi-family
prefabricated housing
project; in fact, the
city only boasts one
other prefab build-
ing that dates to
the 1960s. There are
a number of munici-
pal regulations that
have made it almost
impossible to use pre-
fabrication. I won't
go into that here, but
the first thing we did
as architects was not
to design, but rather
to negotiate with the

**Star Apartments, prefabricated
construction. → fig. 027**

city to make this a pilot project for prefab-
rication in Los Angeles. In that sense, the
invention here wasn't the form of the building,
although hopefully there is invention there as
well, but rather the procedural actions of the
architect before design even began.

The wood-framed units were all built in a factory just outside of Boise, Idaho. They are transported two to a long pallet, trucked here on a flatbed, and when they arrive, cut in half at their base and hoisted into place. There are some cost-per-square-foot benefits, but the bigger economic benefit is that the building gets assembled much faster than usual, and this reduces the overall construction schedule. Also, because the units are built in a factory, the interiors can have a higher level of finish—and these units get a little bit beat up. By "higher level of finish," I don't mean a fanciness of material, I just mean that the controlled conditions under which the components are put together should have long-term benefits for maintenance costs. The interiors are, again, quite functional. You have the essential ingredients of a full kitchen, a large ADA bathroom tucked behind that, and then a bedroom. While the components themselves might be fairly perfunctory, from a design perspective, the overall plan is arranged in a way that grants residents a lot of access to light and air.

Star Apartments, typical apartment interior. → fig. O28

One of the very interesting things about this process is that all of the design and all of the work on the units happens before construction starts. Architects are used to making changes on site, whether we want to or not;

but here, it is more like building a car. The prototype is everything. We flew to Boise twice to look at the first prototype, and then went back to look at the second or "check" prototype. Once you sign off, it goes into production, and you as an architect have absolutely nothing to say from there. Nobody will listen to you. It's on its way. This was a remarkable thing for us, having to rethink our engagement with the design process and the way that, as an architect, you have influence on the work of building.

CREST APARTMENTS

In the time since I gave this talk at Columbia, our office has been working on our fourth project with the Skid Row Housing Trust. In a big shift away from Skid Row and downtown Los Angeles altogether, the Crest Apartments are located in Van Nuys, a postwar suburb of the San Fernando Valley. The site is long and thin, fronting a typical strip boulevard that is unremarkable in every way but very characteristic of Southern California. The project is located here because its sixty-four units are meant to house formerly homeless veterans, and this area is a center of that population in the region. The location speaks to the Housing Trust's ambition to continue to meet those populations close to

Crest Apartments, for the Skid Row Housing Trust, Van Nuys, California, to be completed 2016. → fig. 029

where they are, as opposed to centralizing the homeless population in a very small percentage of the city. The neighborhood of Van Nuys has good public transportation and other services, and these amenities in combination with the on-site services provided by the Housing Trust ensure a balanced mix of independence and support for this particular constituency.

On long rectangular sites like this in the San Fernando Valley, the typical housing type is the "dingbat" apartment building, one or two floors of apartments above surface parking that covers the site.

Greystone Apartments, an example of the "dingbat" typology.

There are a number of practical explanations for this model which we had to deal with as well. As banal as it must seem, providing for fire-truck access and a turnaround in the middle of the site started to define the form of the building, resulting in the arced plan form. This was also exaggerated because, in contrast to our other projects with the Housing Trust, we had to develop a double-loaded corridor long enough to accommodate the number of units projected for the site. We accomplished this by thinking formally of two parallel bars of units with an unconditioned corridor, or "split," in the middle, that allows the two bars to have different elevation profiles and scales. In a sense, this juxtaposition of building scale addresses the in-between character of the neighborhood as it becomes more dense on one side while still echoing its single-family-house scale on the other.

Crest Apartments, two bars of housing split along an unconditioned corridor. → fig. 030

There are two typical unit types at Crest. Both are studio apartment types and variations on other units we have designed for the Housing Trust, but these are some of the most refined and generous, I think. Generous not because they are larger, but because there has been even more attention to the development of smaller "figurative" modulations in the plan and elevation, which, taken together, will have a significant spatial impact on the experience of the living space.

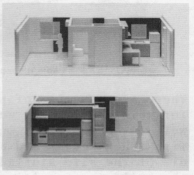

Crest Apartments, models showing two typical interior types. → fig. 031

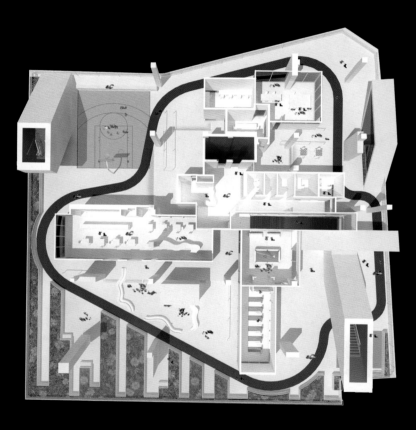

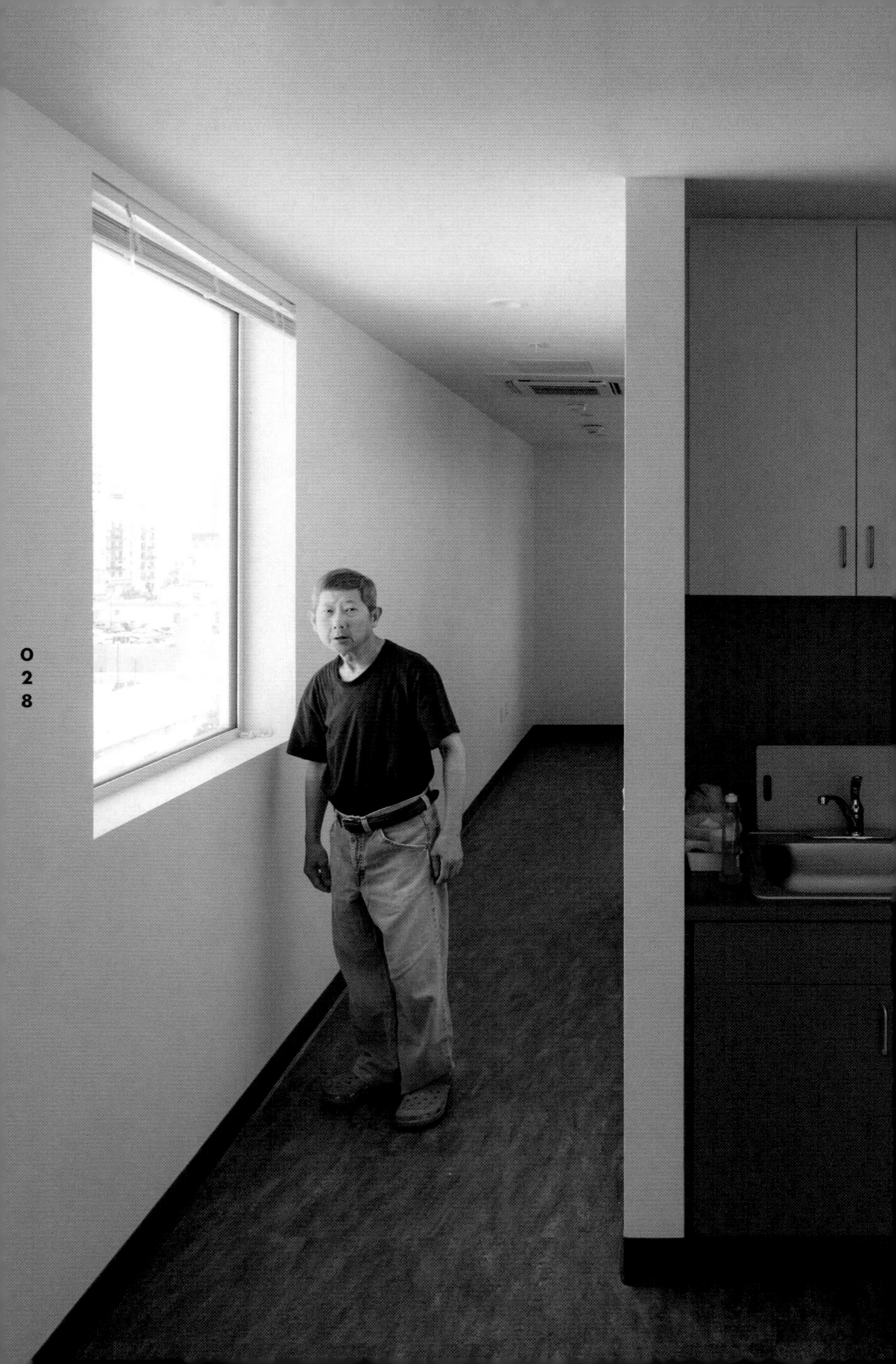

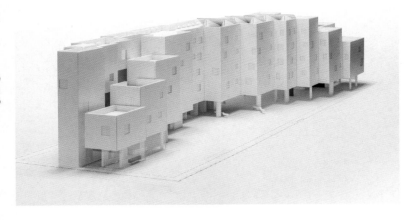

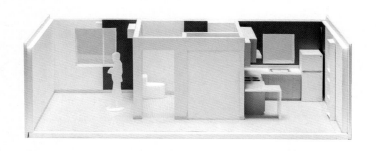

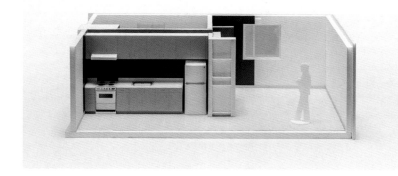

Finally, and with an impact equal to that of the building itself, the new ground plane creates a continuous garden across the entire site. In collaboration with Tina Chee and SWA, we envisioned a landscape that is multifunctional, with communal spaces for residents and a fully permeable ground surface for rainwater filtration bioswales, while still accommodating the required parking and fire lane. This landscape had a big impact on the form of the building, both in the way it lifted the building to become a bridge over the garden and in the way it brings the ends of the building inward, creating at the two ends of the site the feeling that the building is surrounded by landscape while reinforcing the impression of housing that embraces density.

Crest Apartments, atop a multifunctional landscape. ← fig. 032

ONE SANTA FE

Our projects with the Skid Row Housing Trust have all been quite small in physical scale. When people talk about transforming cities, the conversation often centers on very large projects like convention centers, entertainment complexes, glamorous cultural institutions, and superblock commercial developments—projects that almost change the center of gravity in a city. But I think it's also possible to take a more incremental, temporal attitude toward significant urban transformation, and I think our housing is part of that. If you could imagine connecting all of these different projects, then perhaps "the project" is all of them together, with the smaller increments beginning to add up to a kind of remapping of the city itself. This allows you to work more nimbly, I think. The question of scale, small and large, has been very much on our minds.

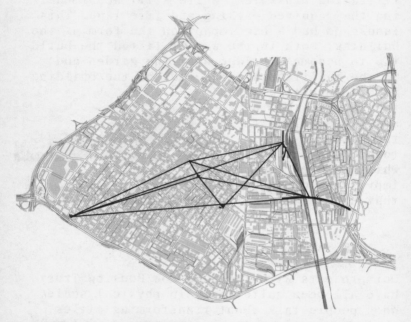

Map locating the work of Michael Maltzan Architecture in downtown Los Angeles, a constellation of projects.

The last project, by contrast, is a very large-scale development in downtown Los Angeles called One Santa Fe. The building is largely market-rate housing, 438 units, with an affordable component of about 20 percent—everything from micro-studios to apartments with multiple

bedrooms, and, in a few cases, two-floor units.
It's also very much a mixed-use building with
retail, commercial office space, and some live-
work housing in the base. The site is unique,
and the building takes much of its influence
from the surrounding infrastructure of rail
yards, bridges, and even the campus of the
Southern California Institute of Architecture
(SCI-Arc) in the for-
mer Santa Fe Freight
Depot. Aside from
SCI-Arc, most of the
surrounding buildings
and train yards are
maintenance facilities
for the Metropolitan
Transit Authority. The
First Street and the
Fourth Street bridges
cross the rail yards,
carrying a light rail line along with automo-
bile traffic, and just across the rail yards
is the Los Angeles River, another type of
infrastructure that is slowly starting to
develop into an amenity for the city after
decades of neglect. From the street our site
looks like nothing but infrastructure, and
in fact many people didn't know it was there
despite the fact that until 1939, when Union
Station was inaugurated, it was the site of
Le Grande Station, the main passenger ter-
minal for the Atchison, Topeka, and Santa
Fe railways.

**One Santa Fe, Los Angeles, California,
completed 2015. → fig. O33**

So this is a big building. Stood on its end,
it would join the supertalls of the world.

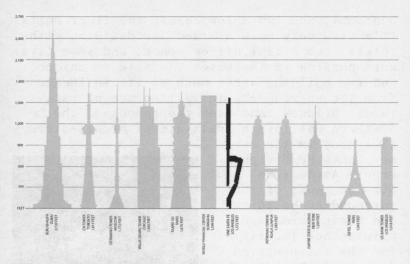

Length of One Santa Fe compared to the heights of some of the world's tallest buildings.

As the building has been going up, it has been commended and also criticized for its scale. I'm used to building buildings from the ground up, but the scale here meant that it was really built from south to north. It's been referred to as a "battleship," a "cruise ship," the "Death Star"—all of those. I ran a studio recently on the possibility of "the wrong scale," an idea that came from thinking about this project's role urbanistically. In this case, we tried not only to carry a coherent design across the tremendous length of the site, but also to break that dominant linearity at intervals, to interject interruptions, rips, and tears with spatial moments that extend into the surrounding neighborhood. In projects like these, I think the ambition should be to speculate or maybe even to anticipate what the

city is going to become. In that sense, I've
said that this project has "anticipatory
scale." It's not trying to meet the city at
the scale of the city today and certainly not
trying to replicate the scale of the city previously, which is, I think, a problematic
tendency. It's a project that tries to use
architecture to project how the city might continue to emerge. As Los Angeles gets denser
and denser, we should continue to evolve and
invent models of what that density is going
to look like, and that invention will be more
compelling if it happens specifically in terms
of the physical, cultural, and social charac-
teristics of Los Angeles, rather than being
based on models from New York or Paris or Chicago or London.

Because of the extreme thinness of the site,
programs had to be stacked vertically, with
the building becoming something of a Neapolitan
sandwich of parking, retail, and housing.
In the wider part of the site, we were able
to do subterranean parking; while in the thin-
ner areas, we lifted it up to floors two
and three, connecting it by spiral ramps to
the housing above.

A semi-pedestrian
area weaves through
the building. These
moments of disruption
in the linearity of
the building create
transverse portals,
visual as well as
physical, through the
building and the site.

**One Santa Fe, axonometric drawing
showing sandwich of vertically-
stacked programs. → fig. 034**

They connect to characteristic moments in the surrounding context and work to make One Santa Fe more of a connective threshold in the urban fabric. Right now the back of the site is given over to maintenance functions, but rapid transit is becoming a more important part of life in Los Angeles, and there's a very good chance that one day there will be a station for this district on the east side of the site. We had some inkling of that, at least, so we worked to convince everyone to allow us to create a big portal that could become a gateway connecting the tracks to the district this station would serve.

One Santa Fe, view from First Street Bridge, across the Los Angeles River and rail yard. → fig. 035

One Santa Fe, building as portal. → fig. 036

Eventually the project might even connect to the river, which is emerging as a site of emphasis in the cultural life and real estate of the city. We're interested in expanding the conversation about what development might look like, not so much in terms of other buildings, but what effect it might have on how we think about the structure and the infrastructure of the city. Since the Los Angeles River is being developed as an amenity, we incorporated moments in the building where a series of bridges might spring off and tether to the river. They could become community gardens, not owned by people in the building, but by the community as a whole. They won't happen exactly this

One Santa Fe, rendering showing potential connections across the rail yard to the river. → fig. 037

way, of course, and they may not happen at all. Even if just one of these happens, it would be an interesting shift in how the city is built. Even as One Santa Fe is finished and people move in, our hope is that the building will keep pace with the dynamic changes that are taking place in its surroundings, and that it will connect to the city as it is now but continue to transform as a platform that has the potential to adapt to possible futures.

Inside the building, the range of unit types is very broad. There are work units, micro-studios of about 360 square feet, one-bedroom apartments, two-bedroom apartments, and two-bedroom townhomes. In the big bridge that connects the structures, we created units that relate in section to Le Corbusier's Unité

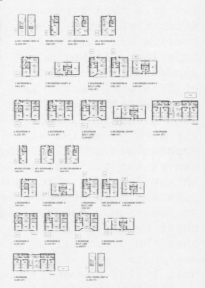

One Santa Fe, interior unit types. → fig. 038

d'habitation in Marseille. There is a single corridor serving units that span the full floor with views out both sides of the building. In these units, there's an entrance floor with a bedroom and office and then a full floor on top or below with floor-through living spaces. We planned for four-bedroom units, which, given the student population at nearby SCI-Arc, might become something like a small dorm to make the building more economically accessible.

The skyline is often our first association with cities since it's supposed to be the most iconic and creative representation of what a city is. But increasingly, I think, architects, developers, and citizens are becoming alert to the fact that programmatic typologies like housing are just as important, if not more important, to invest with inventiveness. The representation of the city needs to include

One Santa Fe, seen behind the Los Angeles skyline. → fig. 039

the work of making visible the city's different populations and their ways of being in the city, expressing the continual emergence of the city in subtler ways. The individual unit has long been the main object of study in housing—how it functions, how you live in it, how multiple units come together. But we shouldn't forget that the accumulation of all of those individual units, all of those individual lives, not only builds community, but also renders a very powerful representation of the city itself.

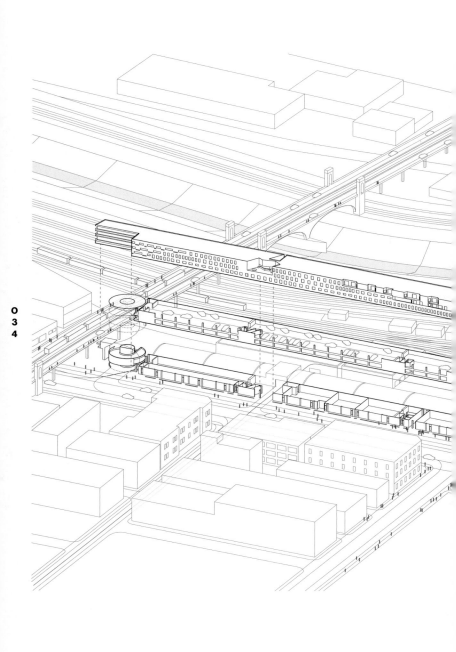

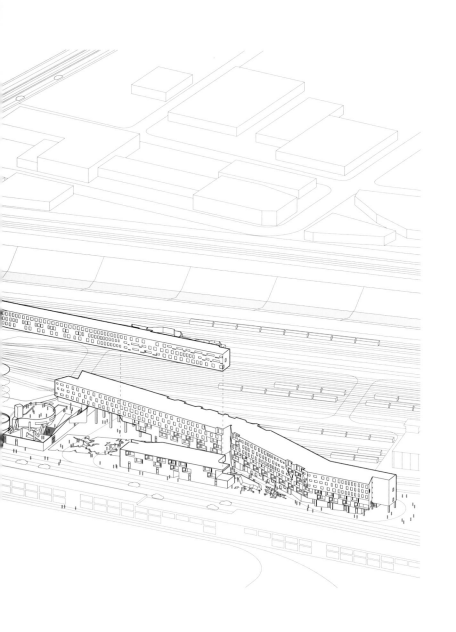

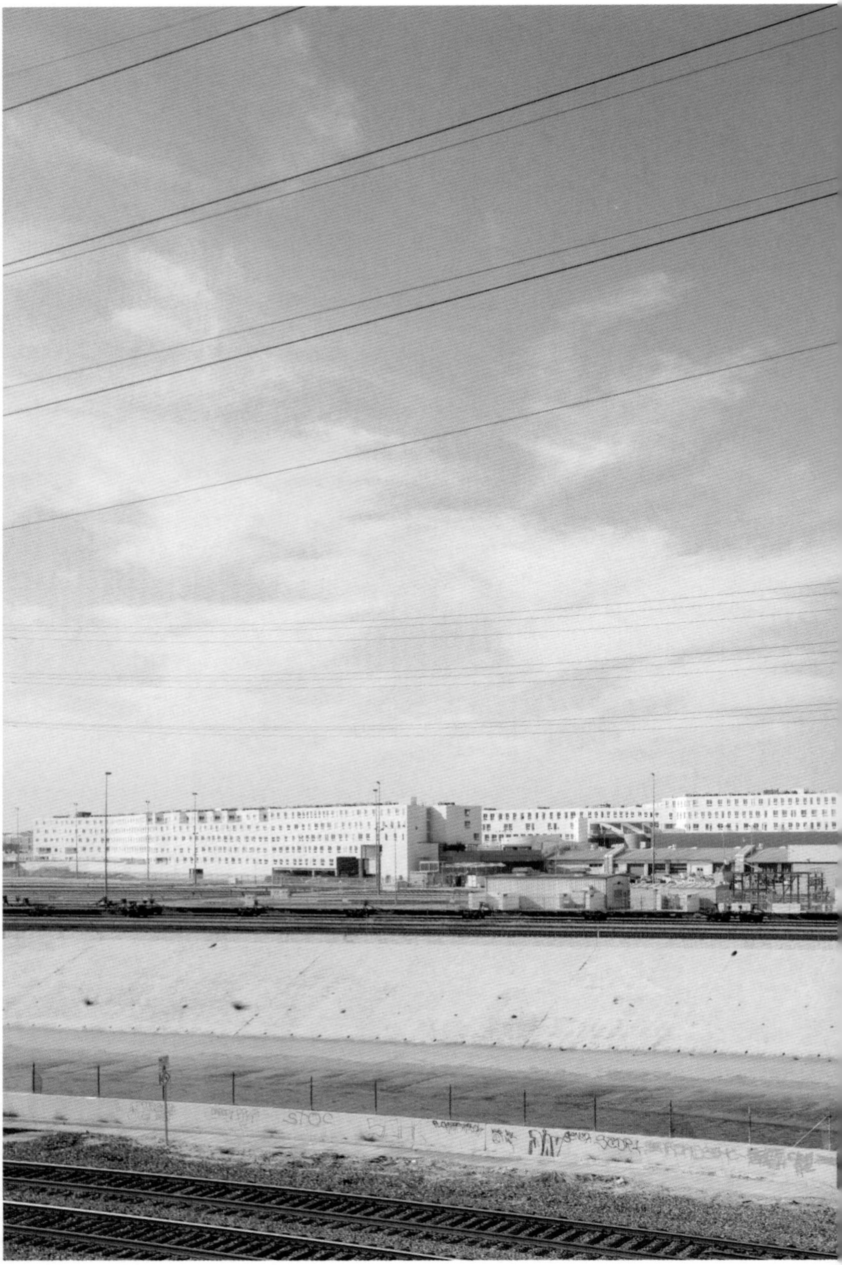

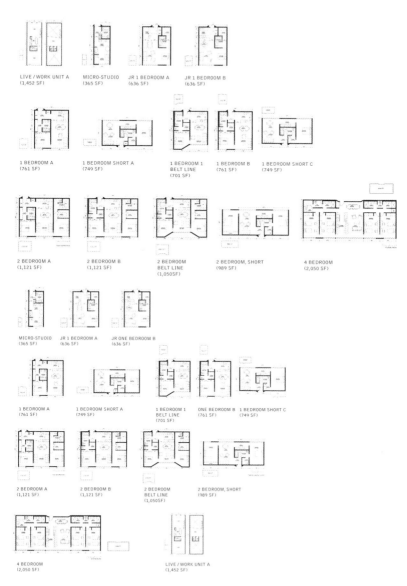

LIVE / WORK UNIT A
(1,452 SF)

MICRO-STUDIO
(365 SF)

JR 1 BEDROOM A
(636 SF)

JR 1 BEDROOM B
(636 SF)

1 BEDROOM A
(761 SF)

1 BEDROOM SHORT A
(749 SF)

1 BEDROOM 1
BELT LINE
(701 SF)

1 BEDROOM B
(761 SF)

1 BEDROOM SHORT C
(749 SF)

2 BEDROOM A
(1,121 SF)

2 BEDROOM B
(1,121 SF)

2 BEDROOM
BELT LINE
(1,050SF)

2 BEDROOM, SHORT
(989 SF)

4 BEDROOM
(2,050 SF)

MICRO-STUDIO
(365 SF)

JR 1 BEDROOM A
(636 SF)

JR ONE BEDROOM B
(636 SF)

1 BEDROOM A
(761 SF)

1 BEDROOM SHORT A
(749 SF)

1 BEDROOM 1
BELT LINE
(701 SF)

ONE BEDROOM B
(761 SF)

1 BEDROOM SHORT C
(749 SF)

2 BEDROOM A
(1,121 SF)

2 BEDROOM B
(1,121 SF)

2 BEDROOM
BELT LINE
(1,050SF)

2 BEDROOM, SHORT
(989 SF)

4 BEDROOM
(2,050 SF)

LIVE / WORK UNIT A
(1,452 SF)

"In the notion that architecture is accessible to anyone, that architecture might return to a kind of pragmatism and embrace of the currents of our time, Maltzan's projects are a casual manifesto for how the city could transform."

L.A.'S NOT-SO-DISTANT FUTURE
Florian Idenburg

Los Angeles, "a city so long associated with the car-oriented suburbs of the 1960s."

Fundamental transformations are taking place within the two main urban centers of California, the state that has been thought to exemplify a model of laissez-faire sub-urbanity. The force of change is a new generation of urban dwellers—a phenomenon found across the United States, in fact—who have a different set of values concerning questions of identity, community, and responsibility (whether social or environmental). The effect of these changes, however, has differed between the two cultural centers of the California coast. A comment on an online forum, which then spread on Twitter, summarized this phenomenon quite pointedly: "San Francisco is a utopia gone wrong, while Los Angeles is a dystopia gone right."[1]

"Our time is one of enormous social transparency and connection to things around us. Our private lives are more and more blurred with our public lives."
← p. 34

San Francisco first. A half-century after the Summer of Love and the rise of Haight-Ashbury as a dream of liberated urbanism—a dream that passed quickly, but which left substantial cultural and countercultural effects in its wake—the urban development of San Francisco is now intertwined with the more dubious techno-utopianism of the dot-com boom and the social disparities that followed. For some this has taken the form of a kind of reverse suburbanism, in which the city is the site of the "good life" of moneyed privilege and private bus networks transport white-collar workers to the corporate parks of Silicon Valley. Even for those who work in the city, this shift has taken the form of increasingly monocultural demographics and ways of living—a phenomenon formerly associated with suburbs and now increasingly a part of overstuffed urban areas like San Francisco.

By contrast, Los Angeles, a city so long associated with the car-oriented suburbs of the 1960s, seems as though it might be evolving toward a more enmeshed alternative. This current idea of the city might well become the model for other developing regions around the globe.

For decades L.A. was understood as an entropic field of enclaves, a mat-city where sunshades and windshields allowed for a coexistence of minimal interaction—a condition cleverly portrayed in the passing-but-not-quite-intersecting narratives that comprise Robert Altman's *Shortcuts* (1993). The city's downtown is frequently transformed into a hell-on-earth in sci-fi movies through natural disaster or simply the catastrophe of inhumane urban development. For years the dark and haunted vision of Los Angeles as depicted in *Blade Runner* (1982), a city of seemingly perpetual nighttime, was an *idée fixe*. Compare

The dystopian, nighttime Los Angeles of *Blade Runner*, dir. Ridley Scott, 1982.

these visions to the magical realism of Spike Jonze's *Her* (2014), which brings us a radically new notion of what L.A.'s future might look like. Jonze's protagonist, Theodore Twombly, falls in love with a sentient operating system (seductively voiced by Scarlett Johansson), but the more remarkable future of the movie is that downtown L.A. is clean, dense, and comfortable. As many have noted, one of the biggest signals that we're in an alternative reality is the existence of robust mass transit, making *Her* something of a bookend to the city's scandalous history of dismantling its streetcar lines. According to *Her* cinematographer Hoyte van Hoytema, Jonze wanted an L.A. of the not-so-distant future, a "world that was tactile and pleasant: the very opposite of a dystopian future."[2]

The magical realist Los Angeles of *Her,* dir. Spike Jonze, 2014.

The Los Angeles architect Michael Maltzan has been con-templating the not-so-distant future of L.A. for a while, leading to his book *No More Play* (2011), which speculates on the city's trajectory in a series of conversations with a diverse range of people interested and invested in that future. For Maltzan, L.A. finds itself at a turning point relative to its historic pattern of growth:

> The city is at a moment where much of the way that it has been developed in the past, which has created both the physical and psychological identity for the city—a city that just continued to push the boundaries outward and sprawl into the periphery—is probably untenable. There is an extraordinary pressure back in and onto the city that is almost overwriting the city in a very intense way.[3]

This brings up a number of important urban questions that older cities have dealt with in the past, issues like transportation, scale, and density. Maltzan's own work focuses on "trying to imagine how you deal with those questions, but deal with them in a way that is inspired by and specific to Los Angeles. I don't think it really helps at all to try to import models from other established or more traditional cities into a culture that has its own identity, its own character, its own spirit."

This spirit is increasingly made manifest in Maltzan's architecture, particularly in the realm of housing. His lines and forms are daring and bold. His predominantly white massings, shaped with hard chamfers and sharp facets, achieve a remarkable clarity of expression in the crisp shadows of the sunshine state. More particular is his embrace of the raw and the given—the reality of the everyday in all its looseness and unpredictability. This engagement with the real, which was also crucial for Maltzan's fellow Angeleno Frank Gehry, results in a distinct attitude toward the spatial organization of architectural materials as well as an embrace of client collaborations that have often been overlooked by the field of architecture.

A part of downtown called Skid Row has certainly fueled the aforementioned notions of L.A. as potential dystopia. Maltzan's projects for the Skid Row Housing Trust offer a form of resistance to that too-easy fictionalization of the realities of the city. This for-profit organization develops permanent supportive housing with a high level of architectural ambition, helping this population in need transition back into a home. The third in an ongoing series of projects, Maltzan's Star Apartments—a daring transformation of a once nondescript retail building into a six-story, 95,000-square-foot mixed-use project—was completed last year. It accommodates 102 apartments for the formerly homeless alongside social services, recreational facilities, and retail.

The construction is of stacked prefabricated modules, but to laud the project for being fast and cheap (as the Los Angeles Architecture and Design Museum's recent "Shelter" show did) is to miss the fact that it proposes a new and important typology for the socially deprived.[4]

Star Apartments, building as city block. ← fig. 025

The most notable innovation of this project is how the apartment modules cantilever dramatically over the newly constructed ground plane of the existing building's roof. The space between this surface and the apartments above creates a new 15,220-square-foot terrace with gardens and a jogging track, alongside a communal kitchen, lounge, and rooms for art and exercise—offering the formerly homeless an alternate ground. Maltzan explains:

> With Star being right in the middle of the city, one of the things that I was actively trying to imagine was what would a kind of hyper-density look like in Los Angeles? I was trying to create an extremely intense, super dense housing block that gets lifted up, and a new type of semi-public space gets created in this layer in between the mixed-use ground floor on the street and the upper level of the housing, as a new kind of ground plane to invent open space within this super density.

Less than a mile away and completed in the same year, Maltzan's project for One Santa Fe explores the possibility of hyper-density from another and very different angle. The scheme was originally a speculative proposal for graduate and undergraduate housing serving the nearby campus of USC as well as SCI-Arc, an architectural school located in a former freight depot across the street. Now the colossal 438-unit rental project has been built on a 4-acre portion of a 32-acre plot previously used for the maintenance and storage of rail cars. The elongated property stretches along Santa Fe Avenue, bracketed by the First and Fourth Street bridges and backing up against the Metrolink service tracks adjacent to the Los Angeles River. The substantial 510,000-square-foot massing—a size that some in the city deemed too large—accommodates a programmatic amalgam of residential, retail, and live-work spaces within the formerly industrial neighborhood context.

"As Los Angeles evolves in ways that the single-family-house model doesn't easily sustain, the city's social and cultural interests are starting to take on a more collective and connected character."
← p. 22

The building's quarter-mile length echoes the strongly linear forms of the surrounding regional infrastructure. Maltzan amplifies this length by placing the apartments in a bar along a double-loaded corridor that floats above a three-story concrete parking garage and over an open plaza, eventually landing on a strip of commercial units toward the south end of the lot. This requires structural heroics that Maltzan deftly employs to give the building its character. The building is not simply an allusion to infrastructure—though it is that, as its formal expression carries overtones of speed and motion. It is a piece of infrastructure in a more literal sense as well, forming connections to the neighboring bridges and offering pedestrian access directly into the raised portions of the building. (Maltzan envisions these bridges becoming still more complex and spanning across the rail yard to the river as the side develops further.) As the project's linear form moves south, it begins to shift, delaminating to create views and ground-level openings across its width for a clear connection

One Santa Fe, rendering showing potential connections across the rail yard to the river. ← fig. 037

to the L.A. River and future transit nodes. Maltzan describes it as "a three-dimensional armature that eventually weaves itself into the city." Interspersed in this connective network are the perks that such buildings require these days, such as a pool, barbecue decks, outdoor lounges, and a gym, each serving as a point of orientation within the complexity of the overall form.

Both the Star Apartments and One Santa Fe are frugal encampments of wood and stucco on top of a new ground. Not hiding their artificiality, they are each comprised of crude concrete structures with ordinary plumbing exposed underneath. They are built to current economic realities and construction techniques. The idea of producing a "second ground" certainly is not a new concept in architecture. In their parti, the projects evoke Masato Otaka's Sakaide Artificial Ground development (1968–86).

Sakaide Artificial Ground, Masata Otaka, Sakaide, Kagawa, Japan, 1968. Photograph by Osamu Murai.

This Japanese Metabolist established an artificial datum over a seismically unstable slum area in Sakaide using a fixed concrete slab and beam platform. The project housed itinerant salt workers in a series of prefabricated housing structures on the slab, while underneath, offices, shops, parking, and a network of pedestrian alleys occupied the fragile terrain. But while this new ground may evoke its utopian or structuralist precursors, Maltzan's approach is not infused with radical rhetorics. Somewhere within the amalgam of new realities of urban development like housing subsidies, affordability ratios, zoning requirements, ROI models, and parking quotas, Maltzan is able to create two projects that are both unique and memorable. Worth considering is that indiscriminate of their users, they are built to a similar unit cost, using similar construction techniques, and equally rich in architectural and structural ingenuity.

In the notion that architecture is accessible to anyone, that architecture might return to a kind of pragmatism and embrace of the currents of our time, Maltzan's projects are a casual manifesto for how the city could transform. They offer models for further development, by Maltzan's own office and by others. Unlike most other cities, space in L.A. is not so precious that development inevitably pushes out less privileged segments of the population. Doubling the ground takes place not because it is necessary to create more; it is the introduction of a layer within the city that can take on novel community or urban roles. These new public layers appear as testing grounds or antechambers, allowing the dynamic and diverse L.A. populace to gradually get reconnected to the environment and to one another. In their scale and appearance, these two buildings have received a fair dose of critique locally, but Maltzan believes they need time. He talks about an *anticipatory scale*. "I think architecture through building form has a responsibility to try to point to what urban forms are going to look like and what the city's going to look like. These buildings try to do that," Maltzan says. If this is where Los Angeles is heading, a "dirty" and possibly magical realism awaits us in the not-so-distant future.

An earlier and condensed version of this essay was published as "One Santa Fe Housing in Los Angeles by Michael Maltzan," in the *Architectural Review* (August 5, 2015), http://www.architectural-review.com/buildings/this-is-the-dirty-magical-realism-future-of-los-angeles/8686180.article, and is reprinted here with the permission of the publisher.

1   The original mention of this phrase was in a Quora forum titled "Why Would Someone Choose to Live in Los Angeles over San Francisco?" http://www.quora.com/Why-would-someone-choose-to-live-in-Los-Angeles-over-San-Francisco.

2   "The Way She Haunts my Dreams," interview with Hoyte van Hoytema, in *International Cinematographers Guild* magazine (January 2, 2014), http://www.icgmagazine.com/web/the-way-she-hunts-my-dreams.

3   This and all following quotations of Maltzan are from an interview with the author.

4   For more, see my "The A+D Museum's 'Shelter' Disappoints by Reinforcing Market Fundamentalism," *Metropolis* magazine (October 2015), http://www.metropolismag.com/October-2015/LA-Living.

"These projects for the Skid Row Housing Trust remind us that social housing should be seen as an architecture of enfranchisement."

IF HOUSING THEN ...
A WISH LIST
Hilary Sample

Models of Skid Row Housing Trust buildings interspersed with other projects in the office of Michael Maltzan Architecture.

If housing today demands that we cultivate a new sense of *social transparency*, and if we as designers seek new models to further that ambition, then Michael Maltzan's four projects for the Skid Row Housing Trust in Los Angeles might help us understand the urgency of thoughtfully designed collective housing while underscoring that to achieve social transparency requires critical thinking about urban living. This means considering the scale of building and the scale of the city simultaneously. In Los Angeles it is not possible to disconnect the two even if it were desirable; these scales are inextricably interwoven. Further, this conjoining of scales points to the constant making, remaking, and unmaking of a city that is necessary in the creation of architecture, as K. Michael Hays has reminded us.[1] Acknowledging this dialectic of making and unmaking is important when it comes to designing housing. In the context of the crowded freeways and the empty concrete channels of the L.A. River, and the city's building boom of new cultural and institutional buildings contrasted with a large chronic homeless population downtown, Maltzan's work represents and embodies this contemporary condition of making and unmaking that is simultaneously happening in the city.

If Los Angeles is indeed a city best understood through its infrastructures, as Reyner Banham and others have argued, then it is possible to say that there is a new kind of infrastructure emerging through Maltzan's housing projects—each offers a series of social services and spaces, and in each case the architecture finds a distinctive, identifiable form. One possible reading of these projects is as a collection of discrete objects. Too often in architecture a building with a unique form is celebrated and duplicated through a singular vantage point, generally the aerial oblique photograph. The reality is that each building is as tied to the ground as it is open to the sky. Today it is important that housing connects that loftier view to the realities at ground level. Certainly these particular projects require a sensitivity to residents that often takes shape in the buildings' interiors, which create places for recovery, recuperation, comfort, healing, renewal, or social interaction. These social actions are enabled through form. It is this approach that allows us to see Maltzan's work as a guide to thinking about collective urban housing.

If there were a wish list for housing it might be something like this:

If comfort is needed, then housing is needed.

If housing is needed, then architecture is needed.

If housing is needed, then it should not be isolated.

If housing is needed, then it should be internally open.

If housing is needed, it should provide visual access to its neighbors.

If housing is needed, it should provide physical access to its neighbors.

If housing is needed, provide spaces for emotional support.

If housing is needed, provide parking.

If housing is needed, provide gardens.

If housing is needed, it should be easily cleaned.

If housing is needed, provide shaded outdoor seating.

If housing is needed, provide a visible entry reception desk.

If housing is needed, enable domesticity.

If housing is needed, enable wandering.

If housing is needed, provide a laundry work-space that is accessible, visible, and has daylight and fresh air.

If housing is needed, provide individual mail-boxes at the entrance.

If housing is needed, provide social support infrastructures that are open, at the entrance and first floor of the building, not hidden or remote. Privacy can be achieved through other means.

If housing is needed, provide small assembly spaces.

If housing is needed, provide access to an ATM.

If housing is needed, provide interiors that are not isolated from the exterior.

If housing is needed, provide a rich color palette.

If housing is needed, provide security and sense of safety.

If housing is needed, then it should be designed in relation to other projects, not isolated from other projects within the architect's office.

If Reyner Banham in *Los Angeles: The Architecture of Four Ecologies* puts forward the idea that the city had grown equally and was therefore equally and easily accessible, then rereading the city today reveals that this ease of access has been largely unmade, if it existed at all.[2] Today it is visually evident that there has been a shift in L.A.'s urban ecology. The highways are overloaded, aqueducts are largely empty, and there is a stark dichotomy between the prevalent McMansions and a growing homeless population downtown. While many cities share these concerns, it is possible to witness the increasing disparity between wealthy and poor, healthy and sick, in Los Angeles's downtown core—a city of sprawl, car culture, art, and design. It is a city that thrives on its investment in novel forms and images of things, people, bodies, buildings, films, etc. Banham posits that the city offered different scenarios of life that were easily accessible to any individual and that reflected his or her relation to the city: "surfurbia" for surfers, "autopia" for drivers, for instance.

Today it is hard to deny that the city's unhealthiest reflection of itself can be found in the form of Skid Row, a neighborhood that is well known in the heart of downtown for its homeless who line the sidewalks with tents and metal shopping carts. While Skid Row houses a population that suffers from a multitude of problems that architecture cannot fix, architecture can at least enable a support structure from housing to spaces for health. In *Thinking in an Emergency*, which poses questions about how we think in the nuclear age, Elaine Scarry describes the notion of a "landscape of emergency" that produces the need for a recognition of "deep principles of mutual protection that consistently appear." This applies just as well to cities: the increasing urban populations who live in suffering need, more than ever, those who take seriously the "responsibility *and the ability* to protect one another."[3] It is a task seemingly too large for architecture alone, but other partners in the making of the city—developers, certainly—should also participate in such a project. The SRHT takes this responsibility seriously and yet does not turn away from design while doing so.

When seen from the point of view of contemporary architectural pedagogy, housing has a vital place as a creative problem within a critical architectural practice. This was part of the importance of having an architect like Michael Maltzan lecture to the housing studios at Columbia University GSAPP, which spurred the making of this book. His notion that housing is foundational to a creative architectural practice, and the way in which he situates these housing projects in the context of his other work, shows us how an architect develops a practice and a way of working. It becomes clear that the housing projects are done concurrently with other work in his office. Even the physical models of his SRHT housing projects scattered throughout his office sit side by side with other models rather than being tucked away or discarded. ← p. 120 There have been generations of architects whose practices developed through the familiar path of first designing a single-family house, slowly shifting to housing, and then creating increasingly larger commercial work, sometimes never returning to housing. Though one can never predict the trajectory of a practice, the importance of housing to this moment in Maltzan's work should not be missed, and it signals a more enduring relationship to housing as a testing ground for ideas about architecture and the city, not as a specialization alone. It has long been something of a truism—particularly in the American tradition of starting an architectural practice—that you're not an architect until you've built a house, or at least that this is one modern path to becoming an architect. Perhaps we might now say an architect is not an architect until he or she has designed housing. And maybe for students today, one is not even an architecture *student*—or someone who thinks seriously about the world—unless housing is part of the pedagogy.

In his first project for the Skid Row Housing Trust, the eighty-seven-unit Rainbow Apartments, Maltzan first sets up the two opposing conditions—providing *security* and providing *connections*—that will unfold further in the Carver and Star Apartments. The project evinces careful thought about design of the interiors, programs and their functions, and a particular aspiration about how the design of a building should engage with the image of the city. At the ground level, Rainbow hosts a series of rooms that are specifically programmed for supportive service providers; the kitchen on the courtyard level and the community room on the third floor can be flexibly programmed as needed. Together these spaces produce new events and perhaps therefore new and different communities; these internal events are in fact more significant than the image of the building. And yet the problem of the *image* of housing is not forgotten here—though perhaps it can

only be arrived at after there is first an understanding of how to construct an interior that allows for a safe and secure environment. Ultimately, though, for this type of housing to serve its residents the building must forge new connections to the outside world and balance that sense of protection with a sense of openness and possibility.[4]

Rainbow Apartments, model showing interior courtyard. ← fig. 009

Maltzan's Carver Apartments concentrate ninety-seven individual studio apartments for formerly homeless elderly and disabled residents around an open-air courtyard. Abutting the elevated I-10, the building's concrete structural walls rise up as if in continuation of the freeway. This in a sense recalls Catherine Opie's enchanting "Freeways" photographs of carless

flyovers and interchanges; her images typically truncate the ground to celebrate the form of the highway, turning away from the ground and purposefully not recognizing the space leftover underneath. Or it could be seen as a space lifted from Werner Herzog's narrations in "Of Walking in Ice," a vividly

New Carver Apartments, ground floor under construction. ← fig. 014

told story of a journey taken by foot: "For the first time some sunshine, and I thought to myself this will do you good, but now my shadow was lurking beside me and, because I was heading west, it was often in front of me as well."[5] Maltzan's project, which is by contrast intimately engaged with the ground, suggests that the open

New Carver Apartments, for the Skid Row Housing Trust, Los Angeles, California, completed 2009. ← fig. 012

space underneath the highway might not be a dead space, but could instead be habitable, usable.

This being Los Angeles, the space under the highway remains unbuilt and open to the air; and yet this openness, combined with the Southern California light, extends towards the interior lobby space of Carver and captures the sensibility of place and environment. The lobby opens to both the street and the space underneath the highway at ground level; internally it opens to the exterior courtyard. These combine to make the lobby and entrance bright and welcoming. After entering through a set of glass doors, one sees a wall of mailboxes, like those found in

Carver Apartments, entry and atrium.

a typical apartment building, that line the main lobby wall. This construction of mailboxes is significant for a housing project in that this particular program of at-risk residents too often has a clinical feel with highly visible checkpoints of security. Maltzan instead emphasizes a sense of ownership and belonging to a community and even the simple but stabilizing sense of identity that comes from being a receiver of mail. It is also a visual reminder that community or the collective resides within.

The architectural form of the building—a central courtyard with individual units radiating out—is repeated over four floors until it gives way to a communal exterior room on the top floor (a formal idea that will be reworked in the later Star Apartments). Furthermore the building tautly holds shared social spaces in a dramatic ratio compared to most housing projects. The development of American housing is typically concerned with efficiencies of lot coverage and gross-to-net areas. At Carver there are many efficiencies to be found (especially in the unit layouts) but also a sense of generosity in the square footage dedicated to social spaces, including the open-air corridors, the courtyard, and the roof terrace. This thinking about moving through the building is evocative of Rebecca Solnit's essay "The Shape of a Walk" from *Wanderlust*. If "artists remake the world act by an act or object by an object, starting with the simplest substances, shapes, and gestures," as Solnit believes, then architecture can be made in terms of thinking about such gestures—in this case, the gesture of walking from city to interior, that *within* there is also an opportunity to wander.[6] Embedded within Carver is also a deepening sense of community—a desire that the community is not just embodied by the building but that it is also expressed in the city beyond. The most evident place that this occurs is in the laundry on the second floor, a thinly dimensioned room painted somewhere between a neon and sunflower yellow. At the end of the room are windows that open to the highway. Here the tenants wash and dry their clothes in natural light and in full view of the highway, rather than being consigned to damp basements or isolated rooftops. It is far from a tired service space, acting instead as a focal point

Carver Apartments, laundry room, looking out onto the I-10 freeway.

of community that becomes in a sense a landmark in the city. The tenants are brought into view of the drivers on the highway and vice versa, a visual reckoning of the "haves" and formerly "have nots" of the city. In this understated but nevertheless dramatic space, some part of the care and coping that happens at Carver takes place through cleanliness.

This laundry room brings to mind a famous black-and-white photograph of Venturi and Rauch's Guild House, sponsored by the Friends Neighborhood Guild in Philadelphia and completed with Cope and Lippincott as associate architects. The building is generally celebrated for its imagery, particularly its iconic TV antenna, suggesting that aging was for retiring in front of the TV.[7] Today our understanding of aging is fundamentally different—rather than a stationary, sedentary way of living, in which the city becomes the backdrop to passive activities, architects design in a way that encourages the elderly (or other populations with particular housing needs) to not be isolated and disconnected from the city. And indeed what is most interesting about the Guild House is that it can be read in this way, too—when photographed from inside, this social space includes

131

**Guild House, Venturi and Rauch with Cope and Lippincott,
Philadelphia, Pennsylvania, completed in 1963; top floor social
room, interior and exterior.**

a carefully framed view of Philadelphia's downtown skyline in a half-moon, floor-to-ceiling window. What is captured in the black-and-white images of this space is a communal sense of place-making that marks a particular relationship to the city.

In Venturi and Rauch's case, the view outside of the window could be replaced with almost any city skyline. In the case of Maltzan's Carver apartments this view is irreplaceable. If ever there were a moment of capturing an urban yet architectural experience of living in Los Angeles, it has to be the laundry room of the Carver Apartments. The resident stands amidst the hums and sloshing suds of the washers and dryers while also standing right up against the freeway's idling cars. When there is a traffic jam, you can make out the faces of the drivers as if you were standing on the street corner about to cross an intersection. Why is this so important? It isn't simply that this is a moment that epitomizes L.A. (though it is), but rather that it captures in a single space a very particular urban condition that is framed, literally, through a social space as mundane as a laundry room.

Maltzan's Star Apartments mixes the urban with the architectural from the first conceptual moments, siting housing atop an existing one-story podium of retail that has been remade into offices, communal spaces, and the new headquarters of the Los Angeles County Department of Health Services. This is the first level of a triple-layered scheme. Above the street-front retail is an elevated plinth dedicated to community and wellness, including a 15,000-square-foot health and wellness center. Above this layer are the stacked boxes of dwelling units, stacked literally in that this is the first

Star Apartments, from Sixth Street and Maple Avenue. ← fig. 023

prefabricated mixed-use, multi-unit residential project in Los Angeles. Here housing is seen as a collection of disparate objects (even if they are similar units) collected together and arranged to form a novel building mass within the heart of downtown L.A.

Star Apartments, internal upper level circulation.

As a city is made up of many parts—that old adage being that the city is a body and as bodies age, similarly cities age—those parts suffer at different times and scales. One of a city's most essential but often overlooked parts is its housing, which has too often been rendered as generic and banal building fabric, something that can be said for almost every city in America today. Housing—particularly "affordable" housing, a term that has replaced the term "public" housing—is treated according to a very basic set of standards and with very little distinction. The New York City Housing Authority (NYCHA), for example, has tended to pursue a relentless strategy of blocky "towers in the park," typically found in cross-, H-, or T-shaped forms offset from the edge of the block with simple brick façades and double-hung windows. This adherence to a uniform representation is one of the universalizing forms of modernism, as if housing in its form alone could be a universal fix or that anybody's particular needs and pains could be fixed through a singular architectural solution. In contrast, what these projects for Los Angeles present—what can be read through the plan of the units and the building section—is that housing is anything *but* universal and that housing (in its exploratory sense, not in its rigidly standardized sense) is fundamental to the practice of architecture. While this text is too short to unpack fully the history of modern housing, one might turn briefly to an example that has been celebrated for being a proposal for universal housing, yet which, when examined internally, suggests difference—for Le Corbusier's canonical *Unité d'habitation* is not universal. The distinctions between each project may be subtle but they are present, and when compounded they produce different effects that further erode the intent of universality. Color shifts on each floor evoke different moods and thus different acts (a lesson that Maltzan has learned as well in his use of color in his projects for the SRHT).

When designing for social transparency, architects should question how program and function relate externally to the city as well as internally within a lot, within a building, within a floor plan, etc. How overlaps, intersections, and superimpositions can link together in response to the needs of a given population or the collective are another site for exploration through design. In these projects for the Skid Row Housing Trust, the prospective residents have already been uncoupled from the city and a "normal" life—they are seeking a way back into some kind of stability and connection. To return to Michael Hays' thought that architecture is always about both making and unmaking, it is clear that homelessness is one case of such unmaking. It presumes that an individual previously had a home but has since lost it, that the normative condition of life would be "homefulness." These projects for the Skid Row Housing Trust remind us that social housing should act as an architecture for enfranchisement. It is here that architecture's intimate relationship to the city, in this case Los Angeles, becomes especially important. To offer this kind of stability and enfranchisement, Maltzan's architecture creates highly specific spaces for residents with specific provisions to the city—the Carver Apartments' laundry room or the Star Apartments' elevated open space. These two spaces provide enclosure for the residents as well as connection. There are specific and revealing frames that allow a resident to view the city just beyond.

While the blankness of Maltzan's forms for the Skid Row Housing Trust might reflect a sensibility located somewhere between Los Angeles and early socially minded modernism, it's important to also root these housing projects in an American history, which has been fundamentally divisive, problematic, and representative of conditions of unmaking. One can hardly talk about collective housing in the United States without reference to the much-discussed demolition of Pruitt-Igoe (1956–72) in St. Louis by way of a dramatically televised implosion, for example. In the context of New York City, a history of disinvestment in NYCHA housing stands in just as well for this kind of unmaking. The history of unmaking is one that we must reckon with, but what is needed beyond that awareness of history is new references that are groundbreaking, that propose a project of making. In that way Michael Maltzan's housing projects write a new history for housing urban America.

1   K. Michael Hays, "Architecture's Appearance and the Practices of Imagination," *Log* 37 (Spring/Summer 2016), 212.

2   Reyner Banham, *Los Angeles: The Architecture of Four Ecologies* (New York: Harper and Row Publishers, 1971).

3   Elaine Scarry, *Thinking in An Emergency* (New York: W.W. Norton & Company, 2011), xv.

4   Nicolai Ouroussoff, "Designed to Help Uplift the Poor," the *New York Times*, February 18, 2010, http://www.nytimes.com/2010/02/21/arts/design/21maltzan.html.

5   Werner Herzog, *Of Walking In Ice: Munich–Paris 23 November–14 December 1974*, trans. Martje Herzog and Alan Greenberg (Minneapolis: University of Minnesota Press, 2015), 43.

6   Rebecca Solnit, *Wanderlust: A History of Walking* (New York: Viking, 2000) 269.

7   See Sylvia Lavin, "Oh My Aching Antenna: The Fall and Rise of Postmodern Creativity," *Log* 37 (Spring/Summer 2016), 214–227, and *The Difficult Whole: A Reference Book on the Work of Robert Venturi and Denise Scott Brown*, ed. Kersten Geers, Jelena Pancevac, and Andrea Zanderigo (Zürich: Park Books, 2016).

Image Credits

Níall McLaughlin, *Street Life*

P. 10 © Ted Soqui

Michael Maltzan,
Social Transparency

P. 20 courtesy of Columbia University GSAPP

P. 22 © Estate of William A. Garnett, courtesy of the Getty Research Institute, Los Angeles

P. 33 © J. Paul Getty Trust, Getty Research Institute, Los Angeles (2004.R.10)

Figs. 001–005, 012–013, 018, 020–021, 023, 025–026, 028, 033, 035–036, 039 © Iwan Baan

Figs. 006–011, 014–017, 019, 022, 024, 029–32, 034, 037–038 and pp. 90, 92 courtesy of Michael Maltzan Architecture

Fig. 027 © James Ewing/OTTO

P. 71 © James Black

Florian Idenburg, *L.A.'s Not-So-Distant Future*

P. 108 © Iwan Baan

Pp. 110, 111 courtesy of Warner Brothers Pictures

P. 115 courtesy of Osamu Murai

Hilary Sample, *If Housing Then … A Wish List*

P. 120 courtesy of Michael Maltzan Architecture

Pp. 129, 131, and 134 © Iwan Baan

P. 132 originally printed in Robert Venturi, *Complexity and Contradiction in Architecture*, 1966, taken here from the 1977 edition

MICHAEL MALTZAN founded Michael Maltzan Architecture, Inc. in 1995. He received a Master of Architecture degree with a Letter of Distinction from Harvard University's Graduate School of Design, and he holds both a Bachelor of Fine Arts and a Bachelor of Architecture from the Rhode Island School of Design, where he received the Henry Adams AIA Scholastic Gold Medal. Maltzan's designs have been published and exhibited internationally, and he regularly teaches and lectures at architectural schools around the world including Harvard University, Columbia University, Princeton University, Rice University, Rhode Island School of Design, University of California, Los Angeles, University of California, Berkeley, University of Southern California, University of Waterloo, and the Southern California Institute of Architecture. He is a Fellow of the American Institute of Architects and a recipient of the American Academy of Arts and Letters Architecture Award.

AMALE ANDRAOS is Dean of Columbia University's Graduate School of Architecture, Planning, and Preservation and co-founder of WORKac, a New-York based architectural and urban practice with international reach. Her publications include Architecture and Representation: The Arab City (April 2016), 49 Cities, Above the Pavement, the Farm! and numerous essays. WORKac is focused on re-imaging architecture at the intersection of the urban, the rural, and the natural. It has achieved international recognition and was named the 2015 AIA New York State Firm of the Year.

HILARY SAMPLE is an architect and co-founder of MOS, an architecture and design studio based in Manhattan, and an Associate Professor at Columbia GSAPP where she directs the M.Arch Housing Studio. Her design work with MOS has been recognized most recently in 2015 with a National Design Award in Architecture from the Smithsonian Cooper Hewitt, a Global Holcim/Lafarge Sustainable Construction Award, an AIA Award of Excellence from New York State, MoMA PS1 Young Architects, and the Architectural League of New York Emerging Voices. Her publications include El Croquis N. 184, MOS Selected Works, and Everything All At Once, the Architecture, Videos and Software of MOS. The firm was a participant in "Foreclosed: Housing the American Dream" at MoMA. MOS's work is held in the collections of MoMA, the Art Institute of Chicago, and Yale University Art Gallery. She has been a design scholar at the CCA in Montreal, and her writings have been published in Harvard Design Magazine, Praxis, and Log, and a forthcoming book entitled Maintenance Architecture from MIT Press. She served on the National Board of Directors for the MacDowell Colony.

NÍALL MCLAUGHLIN founded Níall McLaughlin Architects in 1990. He was educated in Dublin, received his architectural qualifications from University College Dublin in 1984, and worked for Scott Tallon Walker in Dublin and London between 1984 and 1989. He won Young British Architect of the Year in 1998 and was one of the BBC Rising Stars in 2001. Níall is a professor of architecture at University College London; Lord Norman Foster visiting Professor of Architecture, Yale, 2015; and visiting Professor University of California Los Angeles, 2012–2013. He is a Member of the Architectural Review Editorial Board and an Honorary Royal Designer of Industry.

FLORIAN IDENBURG is a founding partner of SO-IL, an internationally acclaimed architecture studio based in New York, and an Associate Professor in Practice at the Harvard Graduate School of Design. In partnership with Jing Liu, SO-IL was envisioned in 2008 as a creative catalyst involved in all scales and stages of the architectural process. With roots in Europe, China and Japan—and sharing the optimism for architectural feasibility typical in those countries—the firm operates in the zone between academia and practice. Recognition for their work is manifested through numerous prizes such as the MoMA PS1 Young Architects Program as well as the AIA NY Young Practices Award, both in 2010.

JAMES GRAHAM is the Director of Publications at Columbia University's Graduate School of Architecture, Planning, and Preservation, where he also teaches and is completing his Ph.D. He is the founding editor of the Avery Review.

Acknowledgements

I would like to thank our collaborators, the Skid Row Housing Trust, Lari Pittman and Roy Dowell, and One Santa Fe Partners, who gave us the opportunity to explore and expand the fundamental conversation about housing and the city in these projects.

Thank you to Denise Bratton and Iwan Baan for their essential contributions to this book.

Special thanks to Tim Williams, Jennifer Lathrop, Genevieve Pepin, and the office of Michael Maltzan Architecture.

—M.M.

EDITOR
James Graham

SERIES DESIGN
Neil Donnelly &
Stefan Thorsteinsson

VOLUME DESIGN
Neil Donnelly

COPY EDITOR
Walter Ancarrow

PRINTER
Shapco Printing Inc.
Minneapolis, MN

☒

COLUMBIA BOOKS ON
ARCHITECTURE AND THE CITY
An imprint of the Graduate
School of Architecture,
Planning and Preservation
Columbia University
1172 Amsterdam Ave.
407 Avery Hall
New York, NY 10027

Visit our website at
arch.columbia.edu/books

Columbia Books on
Architecture and the City
are distributed by
Columbia University Press
at cup.columbia.edu

This book has been produced
through the Office of the
Dean, Amale Andraos, and
the Office of Publications.

ISBN 978-1-941332-19-1

LIBRARY OF CONGRESS
CATALOGING-IN-PUBLICATION DATA
Names: Maltzan, Michael. |
Columbia University. Graduate
School of Architecture,
Planning, and Preservation.
Title: Social transparency :
projects on housing / by
Michael Maltzan ; with essays
by Florian Idenburg, Niall
McLaughlin, and Hilary Sample
; introduction by Amale
Andraos ; edited by James
Graham.
Description: New York :
Columbia Books on
Architecture and the City,
2016. | Series: GSAPP
transcripts | Includes
bibliographical references
and index.
Identifiers: LCCN 2016032616 |
ISBN 9781941332191 (alk.
paper)
Subjects: LCSH: Housing--
California--Los Angeles. |
Apartment houses--California
--Los Angeles. | Architecture
and society--California--
Los Angeles. | Skid Row
Housing Trust. | Los Angeles
(Calif.)--Buildings,
structures, etc.
Classification: LCC
HD7287.6.U52 C27 2016 |
DDC 363.509794/93--dc23
LC record available at
https://lccn.loc.gov/
2016032616